MEGHAN Markle

by Golriz Golkar

BRIGHT IDEA BOOKS

CAPSTONE PRESS

a capstone imprint

FRANKLIN PARK
PUBLIC LIBRARY DISTRICT
10311 GRAND AVENUE
FRANKLIN PARK, IL 60131

WITHDRAWN

Bright Idea Books are published by Capstone Press
1710 Roe Crest Drive, North Mankato, Minnesota 56003
www.mycapstone.com

Copyright © 2019 by Capstone Press, a Capstone imprint. All rights reserved. No part of this publication may be reproduced in whole or in part, or stored in a retrieval system, or transmitted in any form or by any means, electronic, mechanical, photocopying, recording, or otherwise, without written permission of the publisher.

Library of Congress Cataloging-in-Publication Data
Library of Congress Cataloging-in-Publication Data is available on the Library of Congress website.
ISBN: 978-1-5435-4127-4 (library hardcover)
ISBN: 978-1-5435-4167-0 (eBook PDF)

J-B
MARKLE
460-3893

Editorial Credits
Editor: Mirella Miller
Designer: Becky Daum
Production Specialist: Ryan Gale

Photo Credits
AP Images: KGC-55/STAR MAX/IPx, cover; Getty Images: George Pimentel/Getty Images Entertainment, 12; Newscom: D. Myles Cullen/ZUMA Press, 19, INB/Ivan Nikolov/WENN, 20–21, Mark Doyle/Splash News, 11, Matrix/ZUMA Press, 6, Nathan Denette/ZUMA Press, 26–27, P0009/picture alliance, 22–23, ROTA/i-Images/Polaris, 24–25; Rex Features: Rex/Shutterstock, 5; Shutterstock Images: Alohaflaminggo, 31, Dfree, 15, 28, Kathy Hutchins, 9, 16

Design Elements: iStockphoto, Red Line Editorial, and Shutterstock Images

TABLE OF CONTENTS

CHAPTER 1

A ROYAL Wedding

Meghan Markle stepped out of the black car. People straightened the long **train** of her white gown. She climbed the steps to the church. It was May 19, 2018.

She was getting married!

Markle married Prince Harry of Great Britain. After, the couple rode a **carriage**. More than 100,000 people crowded the streets. Photographers took their pictures. The royal family welcomed her.

Markle waved to the crowd on her wedding day.

5

Prince Harry and Meghan Markle posed for photos after announcing their engagement.

MEETING FOR THE FIRST TIME

Markle and Prince Harry met in 2016. A friend introduced them. It was love at first sight.

AMERICAN ROYALTY

Meghan Markle is the first American to marry a British royal since 1937.

Markle was famous before she met Prince Harry. She was an actor. She starred in movies and TV shows. But she also helps others. Women's rights are important to her. She has many talents and helps many people.

Markle is a woman of many talents.

6

CHAPTER 2

CALIFORNIA Girl

Markle grew up in California. Her mother is African American. Her father is white. This was not common in her neighborhood. Markle looked different from the other kids in her neighborhood. Sometimes she felt sad. But her parents cheered her up.

They were proud of their **biracial** family. They were loving parents. Markle had a happy family life.

Markle's childhood led her to many accomplishments later in life.

project

Our mission is to c...
improving the self-es...
young girls, to help t...
their full, amazing...

Markle continues to use her voice as an adult to speak for girls and women.

FINDING HER VOICE

Markle has always cared about human rights. She saw a soap ad at age 11. The ad said cleaning was a woman's job. Markle knew the ad was unfair. She wrote a letter saying the ad was **sexist**. She sent it to the soap company. The company listened. It changed the ad. Markle was happy. She knew then that her voice could be heard.

CHAPTER 3

A RISING Star

Markle enjoyed studying theater in college. She wanted to become an actor. But school was important to her. She studied hard at school. She also went to many **auditions**. Markle got her first acting role in 2002. She appeared on TV!

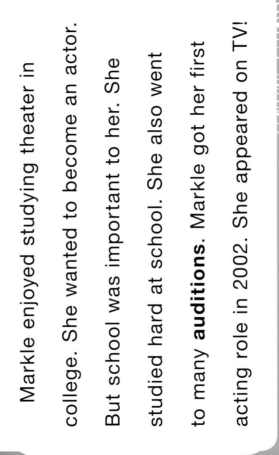

She landed more TV roles. She also appeared in movies. But none were her dream acting role.

Markle had many acting roles before finding the perfect fit.

Markle, center, appeared with her *Suits* costars at an event.

SIDE BUSINESS

Markle needed money between acting jobs. So she found work creating handmade cards.

GETTING HER BIG BREAK

Markle landed her biggest role in 2011. She joined the TV show *Suits*. Markle was excited. It was her first permanent TV role.

She loved her character, Rachel Zane. Zane was a **paralegal**. Markle thought Zane was a smart character. The producers respected Markle's biracial background. Markle was proud to play a smart woman of color. This role made her famous.

CHAPTER 4

A PASSION FOR HUMAN Rights

Markle enjoyed acting. But she also cared about human rights. She wanted to stop **inequality**. Markle wrote an essay in 2015. She talked about being biracial.

She said people should be proud of who they are. She said people should respect each other's differences.

Markle has done many things to help other people, including visiting soldiers.

19

Markle gave a speech at a UN Women's event in 2015.

20

In 2015, Markle gained a special title. The **United Nations** (UN) named her a women's **advocate**. She gave speeches at women's events. She defended women's rights. She wrote more essays.

BLOGGING

Markle wrote a blog, The Tig. It covered food, travel, and a healthy lifestyle. It ended after her engagement to Prince Harry.

Markle visited Rwanda in 2016.

She worked on a clean water project.

Then she wrote about her trip. She said
it was important to help people in need.

Markle helped get clean water to villages in Rwanda.

23

BECOMING A ROYAL

Markle and Prince Harry became engaged in 2017. She left her TV show. Then she moved to Great Britain. Markle began preparing for her new royal life.

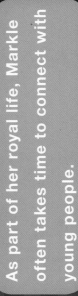

As part of her royal life, Markle often takes time to connect with young people.

Markle and Prince Harry both support human rights. They will continue to help people all over the world.

Markle and Prince Harry made an appearance together after first meeting.

GLOSSARY

advocate
a person who defends a specific cause

auditions
an interview for a role as an actor, singer, musician, or dancer

biracial
being a member of two different racial groups

carriage
a wheeled vehicle that is usually pulled along by horses

inequality
the condition of not being equal

paralegal
a person trained in the law who typically works with lawyers

sexist
showing discrimination or prejudice on the basis of sex (male or female)

train
material attached to the back of a dress that trails along the ground

United Nations
an international organization that promotes peace and security

TIMELINE

1981: Meghan Markle is born.

2002: Markle appears on her first TV show, *General Hospital.*

2003: Markle graduates from Northwestern University School of Communication.

2011: Markle lands her most famous role on the TV show *Suits.*

2015: Markle writes her first major magazine essay for *Elle* magazine on the topic of biracial identity.

2016: Markle visits Rwanda to support World Vision's Clean Water campaign.

2018: Markle marries Prince Harry on May 19.

ACTIVITY

BE A HUMAN RIGHTS ADVOCATE!

Meghan Markle is an advocate for many human rights causes, and she has written several essays that share her feelings. If you could write a magazine essay about an issue that is important to you, what would it be about? Think of a problem in our society that you would like to solve. Why do you think the problem exists? What do you think people can do to fix it? Write an essay explaining the problem, how you feel about it, and what can be done to solve it. Share the essay with family and friends.

31

FURTHER RESOURCES

Love learning about Meghan Markle? Learn more here:

An Essay by Meghan Markle
http://www.elleuk.com/life-and-culture/news/a26855/more-than-an-other/

Krajnik, Elizabeth. *Meghan Markle: American Royal.* New York: Enslow, 2019.

Want to find out more about the British royal family? Check these out:

DK Find Out! Kings and Queens
https://www.dkfindout.com/uk/history/kings-and-queens/

Lee, Sally. *Princes and Princesses.* North Mankato, MN: Capstone, 2013.

The Royal Family: Prince Harry
https://www.royal.uk/search/prince-harry

INDEX

W9-AWN-035

FRANKLIN PARK PUBLIC LIBRARY

3 1316 00460 3893

WITHDRAWN

FRANKLIN PARK PUBLIC LIBRARY

FRANKLIN PARK, IL.

Each borrower is held responsible for all library
material drawn on his card and for fines accruing on
the same. No material will be issued until such fine
has been paid.

All injuries to library material beyond reasonable
wear and all losses shall be made good to the
satisfaction of the Librarian.

Replacement costs will be
billed after 42 days overdue.